The Fleurieu Peninsula
South Australia

Text by Cil Dobré
Photography by Pete Dobré

National Library of Australia Cataloguing-in-Publication Data:
Dobré, Cil.
The Fleurieu Peninsula: South Australia
ISBN 9780957706385
1. The Fleurieu Peninsula (S. Aust.) - Description and travel.
2. The Fleurieu Peninsula (S. Aust.) - Pictorial works.
I. Dobré, Pete, 1958- . II. Title.
919.4232

Published and distributed by Pete Dobré's Oz Scapes
P.O. Box 305, Happy Valley, South Australia, 5159, Australia
Email: ozscapes@chariot.net.au   Phone/Fax: +61 8 8270 5557
Website: www.petedobre.com

Photographs copyright © 2007 by Pete Dobré
Text copyright © 2007 by Cil Dobré
Printed in China

Front Cover: McLaren Vale, Knights Beach, Second Valley and Horseshoe Bay
Title Page: McLaren Vale

Behind every act of creation lies the Creator.

Books Available in Panoramic Series

Australia

The Simpson Desert in Outback Australia

The Fleurieu Peninsula, South Australia

The Barossa, South Australia

Port Campbell National Park, Victoria

The Flinders Ranges, South Australia

The Strzelecki, Birdsville & Oodnadatta Tracks in Outback Australia

Kangaroo Island, South Australia

Eyre Peninsula, South Australia

Arkaroola, Northern Flinders Ranges, South Australia

Pichi Richi Railway, South Australia

Paddle-steamers & Riverboats of the Murray River, Australia

Adelaide, South Australia

The Fleurieu Peninsula

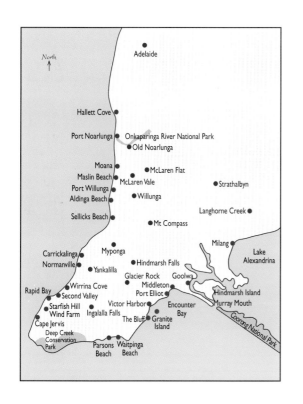

North ↑

Adelaide

Hallett Cove

Port Noarlunga • Onkaparinga River National Park
• Old Noarlunga

Moana
Maslin Beach • McLaren Flat
McLaren Vale
Port Willunga
Aldinga Beach • Willunga • Strathalbyn

Sellicks Beach • Langhorne Creek

• Mt Compass

Milang
Carrickalinga • Myponga
Normanville • Lake
• Hindmarsh Falls Alexandrina
• Yankalilla
Glacier Rock • Goolwa
Rapid Bay • Wirrina Cove Middleton
Second Valley Port Elliot Hindmarsh Island
Starfish Hill Victor Harbor Murray Mouth
Wind Farm Ingalalla Falls Encounter
Cape Jervis The Bluff • Granite Bay
Deep Creek Island
Conservation Coorong National Park
Park Parsons Waitpinga
Beach Beach

SOUTH AUSTRALIA

Fleurieu
Peninsula

The Fleurieu Peninsula

An hours drive from Adelaide, takes you to the Fleurieu Peninsula with its beautiful scenery, attractive holiday destinations, an award winning wine region and a relaxed lifestyle.

The Fleurieu Peninsula is bounded by the Adelaide Hills in the north, Lake Alexandrina, undulating plains, Lower Murray and the Coorong to the east, while the southern and western boundaries are formed by the coast.

The indigenous Kaurna and Ngarrindjeri groups, skilled hunters and crafts people, lived on the Fleurieu Peninsula, before Europeans arrived. Aboriginal names abound like Yankalilla, Carrickalinga, Kuitpo and Noarlunga.

In 1802, Englishman Matthew Flinders and French explorer Nicholas Baudin navigated Australia's southern coastline. Their historic meeting near the Murray Mouth was recorded by naming Encounter Bay. The establishment of two whaling stations 35 years later, sadly brought unrestrained slaughter, until 1864.

Driving the peninsula rewards you with spectacular lookouts and views, with shaded gums, rolling hills, coastline and vineyards in patterned formations.

Inspired by the natural beauty, many creative people settle here. Numerous galleries, like Dridan Fine Arts and Fleurieu Showcase at McLaren Vale, art exhibitions and weekend craft markets are prevalent, selling original pieces of art and locally produced quality crafts.

Over 15 000 kilometres of nature trails lead through natural scrubland, past thunderous seas and towering sand dunes, near sleepy coves, over rolling hillsides and alongside breathtaking seascapes.

A Mediterranean climate with cool winters and warm to hot, dry summers encourages a leisurely lifestyle. Some of Australia's finest, white sand beaches border Gulf St. Vincent, with sheltered coves, tall cliffs and fascinating reefs. Enjoy swimming at Horseshoe Bay, Port Elliot, and surf at Middleton, Boomer Beach and Moana. Advanced surfers ride waves at Waitpinga and Parsons Beach, while some charter a boat, jet ski or wind surf at Goolwa. Visit the Coorong to view towering, white sand dunes or fish from numerous river banks, beaches and jetties. Dive or snorkel off reefs at Aldinga Beach, Port Noarlunga, Yankalilla Bay, Rapid Bay and Second Valley.

The Fleurieu Peninsula provides attractive family activities. Ride a horse trail at Normanville. Cross the causeway at Victor Harbor, to Granite Island on the historic Horse Drawn Tram. Picnic at Hindmarsh or Ingalala Falls, visit Greenhills Adventure Park and Urimbirra Wildlife Park. Relax on a paddle-steamer, departing from Goolwa or ride on a SteamRanger Steam Locomotive. (Australia's first railway ran between Goolwa and Port Elliot from 1854).

Be sure to enjoy the wildlife. Visit Granite Island Nature Park at dusk, to see Little Penguins return to their nests. (About 2 000 Little Penguins live here). Between June and September, Southern Right Whales often visit Encounter Bay. You can observe them from lookouts around the bay. Or take a boat and watch dolphins and seals ride the waves. Walk amongst kangaroos at conservation parks, or enjoy bird habitats at Hindmarsh Island, the Coorong - a migratory wader and waterfowl refuge, Deep Creek Conservation Park and at the Onkaparinga River Estuary.

Interesting local products are available from weekend markets and roadside stalls, including a variety of organic fruit and vegetables, eggs, almonds, cheeses, olives and olive oil, jams and chutneys.

Special events celebrate the peninsula's produce, like 'McLaren Vale Sea and Vines Festival' and the 'Fiesta.' Enjoy world famous wines from McLaren Vale, Langhorne Creek, Currency Creek and Southern Fleurieu (including Victor Harbor, Middleton, Yankalilla, Normanville and Mount Compass). Restaurants and cafés serve locally produced gourmet foods and award winning wines. Visit some of the historic hotels on the peninsula - at Willunga, Sellicks Beach and Strathalbyn.

South Australia's winemaking history began at Reynella, thirty minutes south of Adelaide. 1938 saw South Australia's first vineyard established. The production of South Australia's first vintage wine occurred in the early 1840's by John Reynell (while the first settlers moved into the Barossa Valley). Early plantings at Hope Farm (now Rosemount Estate) in the mid nineteenth century and the purchase of Tintara Vineyard Company by Thomas Hardy are part of this wine region's beginnings. Historical displays of early winemakers and employees appear in many older wineries. In the 1960's, the McLaren Vale Wine Region began to flourish.

Numerous wineries are open for tasting full-flavoured wines. Each winery has its own appeal, ranging from scenic, tranquil settings to those with rustic atmosphere. You may be served at the cellar door by the winemakers.

High quality fruit for premium wines results from the peninsula's Mediterranean climate and ironstone soil. The principal varieties include Shiraz, Cabernet Sauvignon, Chardonnay, Sauvignon Blanc and Grenache. In the 1970's, wineries diversified with the white wine trend, but the region is best known for its rich red wines. Vineyards cover much of the peninsula and their beauty varies with seasons.

To drive from one town to another, begin at the McLaren Vale and Fleurieu Visitor Centre for information. From there, visit the heritage town of Strathalbyn, to browse antique and craft shops and old streetscapes. Enjoy the quiet town of Willunga - an almond-growing centre and venue for the annual Almond Blossom Festival. Wander through numerous heritage buildings in Willunga.

Have a fun day watching cows race at the annual Compass Cup at Mount Compass. Victor Harbor, the peninsula's main town, commenced as a sealing and whaling centre. Now, this favourite resort with many attractions offers a relaxed lifestyle.

Goolwa, once a productive river port, now entices for water sports like wind-surfing and sailing. Visit Signal Point River Murray Interpretive Centre on the historic wharf, to explore history and ecological issues of the Murray River.

Other attractions include iridescent green, rolling hills in winter, Yankalilla's dramatic coastline, unique rock formations at Hallett Cove Conservation Park and the magnificent glow on the cliffs in the late afternoon sun, at Sellicks Beach, Port Willunga and Maslin Beach (Australia's first officially proclaimed nude bathing beach). Descend into Myponga Beach and marvel at the panorama of rolling hills meeting the ocean.

Various accommodation options range from romantic B&B's, family cabins, luxurious retreats, resorts and floating motels.

Whatever attractions and activities you choose, Fleurieu Peninsula offers a relaxed, scenic location, as you wonder and contemplate the beauty of creation.

Hallett Cove Conservation Park

The Sugarloaf - Hallett Cove Conservation Park

Port Noarlunga Jetty

Moana Beach

Maslin Beach

Cliffs between Maslin Beach and Port Willunga

McLaren Vale Wine Region

Rosemount Estate – McLaren Vale Wine Region

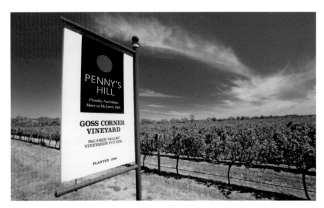

Penny's Hill and Mr. Riggs' Cellars at 'Ingleburne' - McLaren Vale Wine Region

Wirra Wirra Vineyards - McLaren Vale Wine Region

Hugo Wines – McLaren Flat Wine Region

Tintara Cellar Door – McLaren Vale Wine Region

Hugh Hamilton Wines – McLaren Vale Wine Region

Scarpantoni Estate Wines – McLaren Flat Wine Region

Changing Seasons – McLaren Vale Wine Region

McLaren Vale and Fleurieu Visitor Centre

Almond Blossom – Willunga

Overlooking Vineyards near Willunga, McLaren Vale and Sellicks Hill Range

Dridan Fine Arts and Fleurieu Showcase - McLaren Vale

Silver Sands

Sellicks Beach

View over Middleton and Encounter Bay

Surfers Beach - Middleton

Gum Forest on Fleurieu Peninsula

Onkaparinga River National Park

Starfish Hill Wind Farm, near Cape Jervis

A Dairy Herd on the Fleurieu Peninsula - Winter

Looking back to Sellicks Beach, Silver Sands and Aldinga Beach - Winter

Port Willunga at Sunset

Sunset over Myponga Reservoir

Myponga Beach – Winter

Rapid Bay - Winter

Looking over Carrickalinga and Normanville - Summer

Yankalilla Hill - Winter

35

Wirrina Cove

36

Fleurieu Peninsula Coastline - Winter

Second Valley - Winter

Second Valley

Second Valley - Spring

Green Bay - Port Elliot

Green Bay – Port Elliot

Knights Beach, Port Elliot – Looking towards Boomer Beach

Horseshoe Bay - Port Elliot

45

Deep Creek Conservation Park – Winter

Parsons and Waitpinga Beach

Historic Twin Wine Press

Bleasdale Wines

River Red Gum Vats

Bleasdale Winery - Langhorne Creek

Ingalalla Falls

Hindmarsh Falls

Winter

Granite Island and Victor Harbor

The Bluff and Encounter Bay

View of Encounter Bay and Victor Harbor from The Bluff

Petrel Cove

The Victor Harbor Horse Drawn Tram – Linking Victor Harbor to Granite Island

Seal Rock Sculpture - Granite Island

Little Penguins - Granite Island

Glacier Rock

Southern Right Whales

The SteamRanger Heritage Railway – Travelling along the Encounter Coast

Horseshoe Bay - Port Elliot - Winter

Crows Nest Lookout

Signal Point River Murray Interpretive Centre – The Wharf – River Port of Goolwa

Aerial View of Goolwa

59

The Wooden Boat Festival - The Wharf - River Port of Goolwa

PS Oscar W - Goolwa

PS Oscar W - Goolwa

Paddle-steamers on Lake Alexandrina - Milang

Murray Mouth – Looking towards Coorong National Park

Murray Mouth

Coorong National Park